A WOMAN COMBING

12/14/97

Dear Alicia, Victor, Gabriella
and Jo Jo,

"out of dreams of life
perpetuated in many different
languages."

All my love,
Mom (also
Grandma)

A WOMAN COMBING

MIRIAM SOLAN

lingo books

HARD PRESS, INC. 1997
West Stockbridge, MA

ACKNOWLEDGEMENTS

Many thanks to the magazines and anthologies in which some of these poems have appeared: *lingo, The World, Torque, Poetry New York, The Triangle Waist Fire, Monster Trucks, Giants Play Well In The Drizzle, New York Quarterly, Poetry And Grammar, Antanym, Glass Works, East Coast Anthology,* and in the anthology *For A Living,* published by the Universtiy of Illinois Press.

Acknowledgements to Michael Gizzi, Maureen Owen and Ned Depew for their editorial help with special thanks to Bernadette Mayer for her belief in my work and abounding support.

Also by Miriam Solan:
Seductions published by Barlenmir House, New York

Library of Congress Cataloging Information

Solan, Miriam
     A woman combing / Miriam Solan.
        p.   cm. -- (Lingo books)
     ISBN 1-889097-11-X (alk. paper)
     I. Title   II. Series
  PS3569.048W66   1997
  811'.54--dc21   97-3143
                              CIP

Dedication

In loving memory of
Lottie Krinitz Kalichman
and
Samuel Spitzberg

CONTENTS

DEAR

The whole reckoned. Did the archer need

to be shot? My deepest constellation.

Mind the spring. Table the silence

in the resin of my memories. Give me

your unichusetts, your dark hubble.

Is there a you? Which causative

which reflexive? Weigh the suspect.

The quarry of the critic is that

complexity. The absurd absolute.

Go with the slab. Red you can go.

Don't sow by the fender dented.

Bearings who? A wild pitch cons

a caper. Just the big we little

guardians of the pole look up.

DOLMA

In Greek Dolma is
    a stuffed grape leaf.
                On Dolma Road
it's the seasons
    stuffed into a hill.
                Clear air.
Spring doing its green sprints.
    Fall
                going for the gold.
And all framed
    by silence.
                Sometimes a jogger or child
steps into the frame
    or a black dog
                leashed to a man
dressed in black
    talking to the air
                and are gone. Like shells
raked by the sea
    but something of themselves
                remain. A syllabus
of expectation.

    Seems like it's always people
                from other streets
who walk on Dolma.
    Except for several

new families with children
most people here
    are swallowed up in cars.
                Not so much a street
as a lane
    oaks and maples patrol.
                Reds and golds shooting it out
between the sweeping
    hemlocks, fragrant pines or come spring
                magnolias, flowering crab apples
and weeping cherries.
    Lawns and gardens fan out
                mostly sideways
or behind large houses
    about a baker's dozen.
                And all
except for the sister Mediterraneans
    across the street
                different.
Mrs. Gitenstein's shingle
    Mrs. Martin's stucco
                Mrs. whoever she is
just had a boy
    stone–we're brick.
                And like other houses
on top of the rise
    closer to the street
                as if having survived the climb
their antenna bustling Hiya!
    to the dozen crows
                on telephone wires
drying out
    after the rain.
                No sidewalks or hydrants
the dogs don't need them.

Leashed
        they have that three feet
of turf between rhododendron
        or barberry and street
                while cats
contending with no town ordinances
        festoon entire lawns.
                        Happily's the time
I've lifted cat shit
        from round the pond.
                        At least cats kill rats!
as Mrs. Gitenstein said
        in her memorial
                        to her puppy Muffin
caught in the jaws
        of our mutual neighbor's dog.
                        Do fences make
good neighbors?
        The Iroquois
                        didn't think so.
The Siwanoy Indians
        And Village Hall do.

Leaves stuck to trees
        instead of on flower stands
                        in city corners
is that along with
        kids and school what
                        we came here for?
Confirmed cliff hangers
        for two weeks sat
                        on the grass far back
near the weeping willow
        agog

                        at what time had wrought
At cardinals;
            birches shimmying in the sunlight
                        like skinny angels

About three blocks away
            they're building
                        the Taj Mahal
but here on Dolma Road
            houses built 40 to 50 years ago
                        everything's quiet.
The small rhododendron
            that we planted
                        mammoth! Our daughters:
Alicia's in love;
            Samara, testing her wings
                        like the wild ducks
every spring.
            Skimming the tallest tree
                        tops and whoosh!
they're here.
            He, beautiful.
                        She, a frump.
Paddling up and down the black water
            rank with leaves.
                        Are they the same pair
that so many seasons ago
            hatched nine ducklings
                        that jumped into the pond
some too small
            to climb out!
                        And down over the ledge
threw a plank

and like kleenex
                up and up and up
queued the ducks
        the smallest struggling
                    one unable to flutter enough
to lift off.
        Two days
                in, out, yapping
and gone! Save one
        who from every part of the pond cried
                    though I threw it crumbs.
Night, morning,
        mid-afternoon Mother came back.
                    In the pond
on the ramp
        hustling him beside her
                    into the woods
where fat squirrels
        are chasing through the leaves.
                    Snow soon.
How white the sky looks
        through the starry red leaves
                    of the Japanese maples.

CENTRAL

Can
I
make
the
3:11
you
got
a
shot
but
not
a
good
one
and
he's
right
to
the
station
even
the
pines
look
pissed
sticky
and
it's
going

to
rain
missed
my
dentist
appointment
no
umbrella
fuck
shove
over
honeysuckle
and
you
gorgeous
geranium
fatheads
always
so
god
damn
supportive
under
the
dribbling
elms.

Rope

What are you some kind of woman

an hour man she massages you ejaculate

and rush into the recession to take a swim

doctor up any communication between you

isn't there a pile of woman in the sand

towel around me onto the lawn she standing

by window of large picture family about

50 feet out on the lawn up the steps

casually were you expecting to find her

to the a bathroom I had to go to the

her dress on when you had this how-come-

you- aren't swimming on the lawn

Gorbachev resigns maybe that's what

happened doesn't want the union on the

lawn asks can I come in with you late

into the house tired leave already

so now you're saying she can't enter

I tried to enter her you already

ejaculated see we were moving

together hold me down thought

I'd pulled out let's on the lawn did

you her shut up on the beach on the

lawn did you shut up what your penis

in her vagina obviously I ejaculated

thought I pulled out let's on the as

we lay moving already together on the

stupid lawn of me thought I hadn't

ejaculated obviously the bitch had

my penis inside her but didn't have

an orgasm first on the beach a matter

didn't have an orgasm number one when

you say you're having an orgasm there

was semen but I didn't have an orgasm

you didn't tell us there was semen in

the bitch stop moving she got very

changed dramatically honestly said

to my cousin you meet a woman ejaculate

and rush to take a swim back too cold

let's go leave and you go no I don't swim

mislay your is that ejaculate up to house

any you isn't there on the woman towel

she standing by window family about 50

feet up casually were you here to the a

bathroom a her dress on when you aren't

swimming resigns maybe in the union

on the with you into the tired leave

already testifying she starts already

takes her to enter her you see we

were moving me down thought on the lawn

did you the beach on the lawn what your

penis in I ejaculated thought ejaculate

on the already together of me thought

I stupid of me obviously in the bitch

did have her but did not have an on

the beach a matter again went into again

ejaculated having an orgasm orgasm you

didn't tell us ejaculating I get very excited

WHIRLAJIG SAUSAGE

If you're thinking hyacinth why not snow
crocus under a dozen red hot pokers
sprinkling daffodiled greens with a dash
of browalia? Let coreopsis kick off led
by astilbes whose silver plumes boot
a ten yard line drive of Busby shimmer

unlike flopsy gypsophelias whose dimmer
elasticity for long lived riot slow
to germinate dreaming rugged riot shoots
Come-on-snake-eyes! And craps out forget-me-not-smokers
in poison ivy. Mulch and miracle grow ahead.
Mites slug mealies? Spray gnash

fertilize! Which way does the Helicon fly? Hybrid slash
wild avenging stamens inflamed like a hymn a
bove the great squirreled away swatches of dead
red wings in Krasavitsa Muscovy's bright cloud of low
blight and the heaven warped wild leek chokers
for braising winter and colonizing tarragon's snoot

under fiddlehead fronds long as warthogs loot
the panicles of change in wing shaped sepal clash
of the magenta milkwort. Catch sun and acid loving ochre
umbels flip and spackle like a swimmer
through September's salmon rushing hilly toe
of sedum and gifted lilies 900 Simon said

olympic pom poms in a season's hit by Fed
Express starring flick city's honey flute
King Alfred! Cool satin riffs so la ti blow
Alfred! til slightly blue all sigh bash
away. Should farrago toward absolute pitch limber
iris and mind order now to toast as broker

from fall's full to the brim meadow chalices of saffron jokers
gout's 400 year cure on your windowsill wed
without soil or water! to woodland's cosmos like a timber
AhhOoo amid the pin cushion fruit
of lacy blooms and butterflies the weed inhibiting rash
hoar frost pest disease hardy tetraploidy pro

ground skimmer tansy raving mother soaker

pungent bred thigh high sunny smash

in virgin jute sow now!

II Gu-si-sa

Babble on of the numina of the womb of the swamp of the sky

The numina of the womb of the swamp of the sky of God

The womb of the swamp of the sky of God of transfiguration

Swamp of the sky of God of transfiguration of stubbornness

Sky of God of transfiguration of stubbornness of myth

God of transfiguration of stubbornness of myth of whispers

Transfiguration of the stubbornness of myth of whispers of the clay

Stubbornness of myth of whispers of the clay of ziggurats

Myth of whispers of the clay of ziggurats of fertility

Whispers of the clay of ziggurats of fertility of Inanna

Clay of ziggurats of fertility of Inanna of Enki

Ziggurats of fertility of Inanna of Enki of droit

Fertility of Inanna of Enki of droit du seigneur

Inanna of Enki of droit du seigneur of sacrifice

Enki of droit du seigneur of sacrifice of children

Droit du seigneur of sacrifice of children of tears

Seigneur of sacrifice of children of tears of the gods

Sacrifice of children of tears of the gods of priests

Children of tears of the gods of priests of the moon

Tears of the gods of priests of the moon of orgy

Gods of priests of the moon of orgy of the harp

Priests of the moon of orgy of the harp of brewers

Moon of orgy of the harp of the brewers of the echo

Orgy of the harp of the brewers of the echo of Babylon

ARE YOU A GROG

November? alphabet
of mist creaming the
leaf freckled air
as sky fractures it
under the decibels of
the rain nose goosed
I knotted or when
skies as if to fill
in the blanks riot
under maples and
baste it's nice
to be wet to the
yard of our
yesterday pears in
your pocket Mom
pollen off the
larch ceaselessly
pouring

CHECK UP

Grey sheets where are you? Sure this door is unlocked before paralyzed. Once I have it, like it. Where is Dr. Lipman, I'm looking for Dr. Lipman? I'm Dr. Lipman, what are you waiting for? My wife's here. If we're disconnected, get undressed and put on a gown. Anita speaking. What's wrong with her? All the records be right back. What's not wrong with her? Savoring it, that's why you don't want to read. Short. Not on you, all of them. If my mother my older sister would be alive I will tell both of them go to hell. What is your social security number? Thieves and all that. Ask her for an idea. You know I was going sickness, doctor medication and with all that acupuncture they would still be here if all these people are waiting for him. Mr. and Mrs. Growl come back in please. Didn't know looks nice Mommy's car you wouldn't fit in mine. I was home with my Mother, doctor away, small town before Yom Kippur. O.K.? Alright. O.K. Bye-bye. Used to write letters then when they would come–don't lose my place, did I leave a woman's place over there? answer them a big beautiful light so they made a soup in room 3 starved because they didn't feed them. What'd they say?, not ready for her? So they got indigestion. Thank you, you won't be called for a while. My daughter still talking to Dr. Lipman? I'd like to see him don't think I'm her father. A long time twice a week haven't made them the whole family used to a lot of my friends. Should be out in a minute. Take two but break them in half. Breakfast? No such a thing! Put you on some medication once a day with arthritis and with dinner. Anita pick up the phone. Tell him there's a uh really? That, I thought that? Tell me when you do what you do what are you wait wait wait doing? 96, I have to sit here till he's finished with the old people? The other one was in the back also.

Breathe–the answer is no. Don't forget the chart, God and

Revelation on the 18th. Make sure how often she takes

the most 22 a day. Naomi come sit on the table so I can

take your blood. Slowly spring is coming it'll last ten years.

O.K. is he finished with you now? I'll give you a 101 shot. Get

up, talk about it, take your panties off, yes, all the same

thing. Back problems. Well I hope so! You know in the

beginning get yourself a book with some steamed vegetables a

pinch of curry. Anita, where is that left lumbar–hold and

breathe x-ray naturally it's healthier. Excuse one one minute.

Hi! Dr. Lipman. Be with you soon. Stuff to return, so can I go?

Maybe put some body in there. Both too tight. Whatever I say

tell him somebody you know, an x-ray, isn't it a sin waiting?

Dr. Lipman pick up on 2. A good thing you didn't. Be home,

call me. Go ahead. Switched her from penicillin to diarrhea

not more than twice a day careful she's going to get

constipated with a really take it for just but this alright I do I'd like to see you right there O.K. so I'll see where'd she go?

Missing my lunch, Doc. Don't worry, your left reflex is gone.

Thanks, but you're depressing my What I'm going to have

you do is stop breathing But Let's practice You have Open

every back problem known But not ethically right to be

come on operated by a 2nd opinion Sesame stick out

your tongue say ah!

AQUARIUS

Certainly snow banks

and compounds the mountainous fracture

sky tows you along.

Necessity being the mother of invention

Dad came to

on an airy note

that chings in river bed sleep.

Morning tadpoles away.

You are casual as a comma, a pause in a trail

that leads you up mountains

grateful for this breath.

The old woman plays Bach on the clavichord

and the stars strike up in a little water bearer

on the cliffs of Land's End song for the sea cat

licks up the moon.

'69' is beginning to eat you

though what wet heat perverts

clouds with snow, like feathered breasts in winter's

grey flannels, that singing, you wear to scoop the wind,

an air cone

only sunny lips could finish.

Erasing as you go,

the sunlight novel rewrites itself

does not care for daffodils like thoughts

by the spring of green eyes. May

shifts your weight. An imbalance of pavements,

rain paid to the grass

up for grabs, like this moment

and your smile takes.

A WOMAN COMBING

HOMAGE to JOHN ASHBERY

Shooting the blue, the hot lipped Shasta

ascends . The saw toothed Berkshires cut through scrub

    and brush. The staggered Ozarks

pogo away. Chamois dart

    in the crags of the Eagle above the

checkered cloth of hills. The summit

    of the Laurentide toasts gothic bluffs.

Narrowly the Quandary is rising

    like the high slopes of the Himalayas

happened so recently that they are not

    worn down yet. Like the Rocky Laurentians are.

So too the Palisades are a molehill. And the

    blisterdome of the Absaroka an adolescent in

geological time. Glaciers smack the

    refracting Garnet. Deep worn streams of the

Ethiopian Massif pound the tableland: behind

the hammered spear rises Ras Dashan. Footing

the funnelled Split thunder the turquoise tarns.

Fresh clefts rent the Pelvoux. Like the Pinos

but unlike the Liberty where the gap seems to spring

not from climbing the ridge

but of finding it. Orange lichen spring from the

Lebanon. The serrated flanks of the Brochen are

gold, the Andorra snakes into an alluvial flow,

the Bonnet: a muddy cistern. Pikes

Peak massages the blue gums of the sky. It has Niagara

for a mouthwash. But the Adirondacks

gargle blue spruce. The anthracite Sandford gnashes

in snarling darkness. But where there's light

there's oak on the Zugspitze. And climbers roped to

the Viso. Echoes resound

from the Fuego. The McKinley is one

    of the tallest ascents in the world. The Harvard

is in Colorado, rising. Stars

    saddle the crested Atlas

as it posts. The deep ridged Thompson

    hitches a ride. The sinuous Twin draws you

into its purple folds. But the windwashed Orizaba

    is all thumbs. The Matterhorn gives you

the finger. The Big Horn is a Bach invention.

    The Finsteraarhorn is too steep to mount. Go quarry

with the Granite. Thermals around the Misti blow

    boldly. It may grow into cumulo nimbus

during the night. Or like the Oquirrh, sachet

    through river spray

and pine. For the shoulders of the Stanley

    are soft. Like the Mauna Loa, wrapped in sheets

of silt. So what if the Aconcagua's crags sag!

    When the moraines of the Mission

table the faults of the Ghost

    will the Penetentes wait for you? Mishmi? the pretty

Anapurna? The Sneffels escaped to the Telluride,

    north of and the Colorado south of

the San Juan. By the bauxite shall you know

    Djebobo. By three

thousand feet site the Torando

    from the lemonade stand under the electric

humming of the Hood. The Lewis blends

    into the smokey blue haze of the crystalline

Appalachians. The Dickey squats

    in shocking azaleas. Through clay muscles

the Massive expresses itself. And as ore

    is drilled through the huge Mesabi Range, so you can

through the Sierra Nevada, a block

    400 miles long. Radar hums

on the Drum. Here though the Danda Devi rises

    the Titan erodes. And the charred and truncated

Stalin. Olympus too stumps

    like a campaign gone wild

in the eye of the Gargurus. Shall the Caucasus

    strike gneiss? In the col of the Mau?

Can you tell like the Hartz the Walpurgis

    of Goethe? Deep ravines radiate from the summit

of the Morgan and the Valley of Ten Thousand

    Smokes. Can the Bogart slough off

its floes? Tune in the Cololo.

    For the Cacca Acca is deep

as the Pissis is, wide. The Dikte

    amasses conical screes, and the

Empedocles zigzags fissures. The Esposito

    bands parallel trenches

but the mudslides of the Cannon

    engulf it. The Invisible sites deep depressions.

The Never smokes. And the Inacessible

    too, smokes. Many winds blew

a huge drift of snow upon the Dais. Then turned

    to Eolus to behold their breath.

It was nerve gas. Red clouds hug the

    Titlis. The Nu

stakes out the moon

    like Picasso's woman

combing her hair.

MADAME BOVARY'S CORSET

The shushing of the spruces
are like the loosening stays of her corset

as Madame's elastic hooks
into the balsam clasp of her lover

while the salty mattress squeaks
just as the kinky sassafras does

as you nibble between the flaps of my
capricious needling of the pines

IDA'S SLIP

Thank you very much
of 5 little aunts
and not many flowers
and she was close against the railing

of 5 little aunts
if a house has windows
and she was close against the railing
nor was he too stout

if a house has windows
smells of herbs and fields
nor was he too stout
nice dogs often are

smells of herbs and fields
well there was her umbrella
nice dogs often are
sitting and then that was a day

well there was her umbrella
or perhaps 2 in each

sitting and then that was a day
tag to pussy wants a corner

or perhaps 2 in each
hat and every hat was off
tag to pussy wants a corner
count to ten

hat and every hat was off
almost never had been younger
count to ten
every bit of lighted wood

almost never had been younger
and not many flowers
every bit of lighted wood
thank you very much

LIGHT

draws me to this room: the early sun splintered on the peach silk walls. They turn gradually copper reminding me of one of those tremendous heavy skinned peaches in Positano at The Sirenuse that I had to eat with a fork and knife. So sweet and juicy under the stars. Above the sea, below the fireworks.

I smoke. It is my fifth cigarette. It dulls my mouth. The smoke curdles in the slanted ray of sunlight mixed with dust particles against a cream colored ceiling. The paint is beginning to peel on the right side. Under the center beam in front of the window are hanging baskets of pink and white fuchsias, lavender lantanas and Martha Washington geraniums that I have taken in from the terrace for the winter. Though the windows are closed, the lantanas move slightly casting filigree on the wall. The clay pot saucers of coral and red impatiens, flame coleus, wandering jews mixed with snake plants are still filled to the brim from my watering this morning. The plants lean toward the sun from the wide ledge under the window, part of a walnut bookcase and floor cabinet built by an old Belgian carpenter. I cannot remember his name. I wonder if he's still alive.

"Regardez les papillions!" he said, pointing proudly to the wildly grained rosewood inserts: actually the four inserts resemble more an open tall tepee in which a seated figure holds his leg, a gaunt clown with horns, the third a vulva, and the last, a butterfly. I am surprised: I have never seen the butterfly before. To the left is an open grid that I backed with a peach curtain to hide the old radiator. The squiggly brass grill in the shutters is on the left golden, silver, black and green cast under the shadow of leaves. Through the bars the dirty window, the storm window even dirtier: Blanca complains about her back and will not lift the window to clean it, Gina before her accidentally turned on the alarm and afterwards wouldn't go near the window and the window cleaner said the white flecks are in the glass and cannot be cleaned. Old panes. The storm window has two elongated grey spots. Pigeon droppings. Perhaps it is pigeon justice since I stopped feeding them. They congregate on the low parapet that separates my neighbor's apartment, but closer to her windows. Two pigeons huddle on her window sill. Her window framed by the same lead stripping as mine appears brighter probably because I am inside looking out. The lead strips create a broken pattern behind the shutters while the clear plastic alarm contacts along the window side almost disappear in the sunlight. The green, red, black and white rectangular sticker in my center window says BURGLAR ALARM. The sticker reminds me to turn off the alarm if I want to open the window more than six inches. I find six inches allows enough air. I have been robbed twice. I do not know my neighbor.

GREAT MORNING

Staten Island Starters under spandex skies emotions
starting to surge in last minute knee bends East West and
Down Under ready to push off hello Bernadette good luck
Lisa how's your batteries start looking orderly tremendously
organized like a champagne bottle Dinkins the water cannon
and there pop they go seconds off the Verrazano's great steel
ropes Miss Liberty and Twin Towers of the World trade
punches 1126 check him out leading the pack for his
moment in the son of Tanzania winner of 1989 pulling out
near perfect temperatures 25,000 mauling the sky pretty fast
three women in this race really ready to run but the men's
field the runner philosopher from Kenya more than anyone
Peter Maher of Canada most confident audacious fireboat's
official salute whirly birds remember Joan Benoit's great race
in the Olympics 7 years ago very interesting psychological
ploy Lisa taking the lead strong head wind see her hair flying
back and here's Hussein now Ukanga snagging crowds an
endless stripe one race people Fort Green a live and very let
live we were accepted it's our we love turf Russian shoemaker
Dominican take-out shop Italian baker time 43 minutes and

49

14 seconds Ukanga out there running on his shoulder Hussein followed the last five miles by the sun all the from Kenya in the mountains of Albuquerque a very little kid chasing the clock around the leaders through Manhattan Ukanga different serious a surge point growing into a hill develop a psychological dominance over the Queens bridge carpet stretched feet adjusting to change of turf and the seconds lost switch back no one seems to be making the move on First crowds cheers Squirrels from Hell looks like a real blast between the women coming up with estrogen smiling tremendous pace from the Soviet Union Olga running fourth with a time of 1 hour thirty minutes twenty five seconds Samuelson has dropped back is out of it the photo press truck coming in picking up his lead from Mexico into Central Park Garcia thousands cheering trying to assert herself Ondieki improved her time this year in Los Angeles three minutes chances of victory one person has to be two looks like Liz is trying to take the lead flags flying musicians playing this last stretch wind right in their faces bonus money flags the finish line is there a Mexican flag up there go Garcia 22nd marathon she ran smart front of the police motorcycles if he breaks two point nine it's worth 40,000 in white shorts white gloves Salvador Garcia streaks only the 8th man to break a record Espinoza coming in second you know they're dancing south of the border champ second

50

champ 35,000 in bonuses two Mercedes official winning 2 hours 5 minutes 28 seconds now it's Markova making her move putting on the speed McCoogan of Scotland in a surge still on the East side Ondieki's not going to let her go Liz McCoogan rounding the reservoir arms back brilliant strategist putting the hammer down has she a chance perfect control passed 90th and 5th going break away move course record just a second Ukanga still with a lot of guts past champion comes in a zoo gets the water cannon but here in the first marathon Liz the filly she is boy does she look good when you made your move today did you know you'd made the decisive move to break away Garcia after the 17th mile and take it away here at the finish line comes the American Pat 2 hours 20 minutes 29 seconds the local man some hope he'd finish earlier heart problems right now 21.03 unofficially watching Liz McCoogan picking off the men in the field herself against the clock not another woman in sight sprinting really flying past the halfways mark not as chilly another factor top runners at Tavern on the Green in largest race in world prototype for world big city races remember five boroughs bridges 50 bands psyching them on 2 hours 25 minutes Liz down to one minute away don't know the statistics fastest marathoner in history take a well deserved rest this year for the Olympics coming up Enrico Wilson goes

crowd cheering Liz 2 hours 45 seconds Liz in all her training
here on her maiden voyage 1000 meters world champion
raising her arms she comes!

RAP

Legs pumping passing

calabashes leaking

icons of protocol

ambush hunched over

letters electrolytes

a strange urge to strip

rebellion from its sideburns

between aquatic cognac

makers and chorus frogs

used as doorstop

by a copywriter

cut into one inch squares

caveat glassy eyed hug

grunt with hundreds as muck

night volleys harlequin

sky's god damn jewelers

SILS

The tunnel gives birth to our skis

    sails, a whole family of deer stalking the tracks

      bare branches rocking the sky

and behind them pine half covered mountains

    and in between Ziegelbrucke a man

      fishes on the banks of December. Snow

will it or not? A plane scratches the sky

    and the conductor entirely incomprehensible

      hollers in Svizerdeutch at tall birds' nests

in the moustaches of trees, farmlands

    rooked by streams and in between them

      Turkish figs, fresh fat dates and Henry

rustles the bag as Marnie stretches out

    pocket book for a pillow, and Samara

      opposite dreaming, her face bald cliffs

and in between them the green shutters

    on little wooden houses and in between them

        hills opening and closing like the green shutters

on little wooden houses and in between them

    Henry opening and closing

        the paper bag and cleaning each purple grape

in a tissue and in between that stacks

    of wood and smoke

        rising against the hills heaped up

between small spires punctuating

    the paragraphs of houses and against hills

        on one side of the comma, vineyards

and against the colon, tractors

    a girl bicycling and in the opposite direction

        an express whistles between the large iron

hands of a clock says 10 after 4:00

    on the station to luggage piling up

on a wagon by a station hand and after that

farmland, poplars and a sign KLOSTERS

hinged on the wind and Marnie turning

and Samara turning and us turning

the memory of Marion and Claude skiing

in KLOSTERS a few years before he died

and after that too close to the tracks

factory towns and a healthy baby

in the next compartment delivers Tosca

in Chur between changing trains

and blowing my stuffed nose

when one train empties out and our compartment

fills up with luggage on wheels

Svizerdeutch and a young boy dressed in green

scratches his belly and in between

the sky darkening with slices of orange

and purple in brown jeans hears what designers

germinate in many directions street lamps

turning on and the white lights

on a small fir tree and a class in dyes

and a computer printing design

is it lilac or rose between the pines?

and over the silver wing of the lake where

the conductor silhouetted above the train steps

tips his cap to the moon in Swedish

where the little boy comes from

and in between lights in the houses coming on

in the dark like James Bond and the spy

who loves me and in between nights

of the midnight sun confiscation

by the government in taxes up to 75%

knowing how many slices of bread you eat daily

and in between the wagon rolling hot coffee

horrible! give it back and cross country

skiing right from the door of the inn

and in between the young boy sucks through a straw

the blackening sky and in between lights

scouring the tracks grasses swishing

in cold air seeping through the doors

outside the W.C. and in between clumps

of snow and gum on Phillip's fingertip

staging more than substance

amazing engagement of what plays a year older

and in between the discovery keep writing

snow a whole poem Christmas eve real estate

what it is ten minutes before 7:00 in heavy snow

DRÊM

It was green sharp the peep after the
even before. He had none of that Iness
about giving I the hook. Percase the
moment of the couple becomes the
comeatable of either equal forces by rise
of a phall. From side holing strokes
leverage increased in bent and turns in
all of its researches. Feastress of high
feather we were steeped and what my buds
forged his tongue must vent. Lip it, knave,
lip it. Blank me if you think he was losing
his sand.

WORDS WORTH

on JOHN ASHBERY

So ends the magnanimity of the eternal lesson

Ardor need never have excited any jealousy

On your part: a note of fashionable melancholy struck

Such particulars you mouthed, all leading back

To catch up to me in the street, still with the same features

Fresh and full, with leaves and other things flying

As if gossiping squadrons of Inspector flying

Clouseau mistook our volcanic acoustics for their telephone lesson

So amplifying the 'minkey' with a few of their micro wave features

Monsieur, do you still want me to crank it around? Because
    jealousy

Has already moved us toward and further back

However this new stance hasn't prevented us from being struck

In the mulberries of this old country road. Struck

Plucked and forked. With the resultant dislocation flying

Into ingenious shifts like unheard guarantees of money-back

Ladies all rouged up into the decollete night of the lesson

We see it all now. Transposed into the minor key of jealousy

Just as your Mother warned you it would when your features

Froze. That inquiring look that a dart features

Will creep tired and enraged into a bed struck

And straggly. That the blue of the sky is a little jealousy

In all directions history must move very fast to stay flying

You forget the slightly bitter lesson?

The sagging whiff of nostalgia back

In the blue print stage? Remnants of the old back

And not the movement of the fall burnish perpetually colorless
    features

Suck up the sun in every pore of the lesson

That our actions straining all our lives struck

Perhaps others in the clutter will bend flying

Under the off shore baton such arpeggios of jealousy

Gradually peeling away as wallpaper or light to keep jealousy

From going blind. Utter rebuttal of the back

Tracking rehabilitating sunset. Imagine the compass flying

Eyebrow buffeted by invisible winds that don't tear us to features

Always and nowhere a cave but like Plato struck

By his own earnestness in hope and cold as if letters pumice the
    lesson

That that callous jealousy hands out. You see how no design
    sticks the lesson

To underline the paradox of its flying, as if the 'as if' features

Lightning behind your back a deal that rain's small hands on the
    hour struck

MNEMOSYNE

The branches of intense vessels
as the moon moves the egg ripens
and the uterus blooms: cabbage roses.
Thorns tide the legs and tendrils
in the mind open

vodka of blue rivers
wingless arterioles of an interior sky
clinkers of black smoke-stacks on a rocking
ship in a crucified sea
which the bushed shore scribbles:

pomegranate red, amaryllis red, robin red, terra cotta red,
    Venetian red.
Fire engine of blood, prana pump, brain bank, mill and
    unconscious press

blood is my ink.

THE PINOCCHIO PAPERS

FOR BERNADETTE MAYER

1

It was raining and going to rain. Martians in one ear
pictures from an inhibition in the other. Can you saw
off this hole of minutes and set it afloat? Prepare for
wake shouted the captain as if were not so much the
sea's convulsions. Out on a suburban limb washing itself
a dying fly's feet tangle in a mimicry of graffiti.
Pinocchio I want Pinocchio! growled the little tiger
tearing the pages out of the woods.

2

Recycling into it yes there is tripe. Wound up for her
maiden here in yellow frazzle the if only bird. The way
today is schlepping along the clouds need arches. Night
old swivel hips shall we let a few whores get the better of
us? Autumn twirled its mustache from a huge distance
and I marsh. That little red thing flapping in the grasp
roots was her tongue.

3

I want to penetrate you. Coming up is our heading of 337
degrees and we were supposed to be on it. Oh to be a bird
and shit on everything. You don't want me to sit in front
said Pinocchio, Huhh have to do with it. The view I don't
understand what you're saying in the living room everyone is in
front but when you're traveling at home do we sit in front what
is it about here the view in front when you're traveling you
decide you control you manipulate. How incredible bird
index finger size grape vine sprouts. Trees upright dry cycle in
the general electric.

4

How could I have left in the middle of the future? Now you
have to turn two things to get the cork out. Poppy and
memory. Is this all the blood I'm going to squeeze out of these
turnips? Will you keep tired I am still shut up? You don't get
sleep. You're only good for target practice. Exhortations to
nation to keep at eye level rather than high like a scud. Day
and night bells can't they wait. Don't be intimidated they
seen you sitting here way back on chairs like to be sat on
that's why it's a thing somebody made it. On what table
according to what grid of identities or analogies have we
become accustomed to sort out so many different and similar
things?

5

Breeze faxes the white flowers. God bless you spring.
What I like about Valesquez is his tone and fastidiousness.
Slats up a sleeve what are the cut offs of your
options? Can I catch up to my life? Pity moves her.
Wanted not him but the thought of him. Have I forgotten
a part and parcel? Where is my nib my white soul?
Linkage bothers you would have happened if it wouldn't
flush?

6

It's a logistical sky. Good I'm good for you? Open your
wings let the moon out. A new boom sweeps clean. All
the better to plays with her nipple like a baby playing
with a button in a button hole. Let us go step by what
total damage is it exists you pay for it. Some pelicans
dive from great heights this one didn't want to show off.
Here sir fire eat!

I Am In Bed With You

Foreplay, a song, we stave the darkness
like the ribs of a tent

I am in bed with you long distance

I will give you your party. My tongue
is yeast your little loaf rises
the mirror breaks out you are taking off
the sandy suit from San Marco
with a gondolier underneath
                    blizzard of words
                    we with our oars
your ribs are poking me meat hooks
they used to hang up children
                    the age is full of lies
                    lampshades, soap, humankind
cannot bear such sheer buggery
up the annals of war. Ooh ooh me and do me
tender, like a phrase coined you pay
with your life
raspberries embarrassed and blackberries

I am in bed with you between a curve and button

is a little footpath that mounts more
than glass. feel we feel, feel so much.

no oyster closer.
                    the world
                    what are we doing

a catharsis: I am in bed with you
yes two million dollar ransom I am in bed with you

without coils of excuses
the slums are rising
yes in black and white tunnels
are being blown

yes the war is invisible I am in bed with you

our bones are crumbs
we are rolling in
you are wearing a medal for praying
yes we are the only angels that exist

faithless I am in bed with you
                    yes hawk, yes jelly, yes site yes
                    bullfire
                    America is coming

I am in bed with you

SOMETHING ELSE

Queuing up because this is

the show in black and white.

I promised Marlene life, Henry promised me

and yesterday's stunts into morning, hold on-

there is time for the wind to blow its stuff,

throw your head back and gravitate toward center

where is the pull and spill of a green fountain.

It will filter through that screen definite as soot.

The siren sounds. You don't live there anymore.

A game of touch and going on rain that pumps the

mouth root. Creep up hills. Will the trees

of grass tell you something? To wear lilacs

as a face. As if love was Sophia you could top

with a hand. Independent as the seed raking

the water that ripples before it spills.

Jerking around on a possibility's tail.

What matters is up ahead with the scout bareback

on his white mare breathing out on a snowy

mountain. We are nearing the middle.

Wouldn't it be wonderful say, if there were a

renaissance of the human heart? Laugh, but

TENDER BUTTONS is just another idea, closely

fitted, wearing mostly a smile. Sincerity, a hybrid

daisy, never quite sure how it will end up.

These cobblestones have run away into the alleys

of beaded curtains where the refracted light

threads the squinting eye. Masters

of the 20th century kill and overkill

yet something in between like a long drag

on a cigarette to tally up the cost of living.

A stalemate, the queen is dead, but never to

underestimate the next step of a pawn

in the 7th rank. Stagey business. Shooting it out

on the other side. Still there is no tragedy

unless you succumb to a fatal flaw. Distracted

by the red moon, but the show goes on.

CODA

From adagio to barge now York fiddles

in the wind-eye. Conjecture scrapes

a cloud from what is now. Originally

what stood between two and twain

was only gender. But when men dialogue

with their noses, their communication

is smoke. Planca, also nasalized from

the base plac exudes placenta. Of the

tasteless and invisible all land

animals breathe. Aere the aire

the river Mozart pants!

SONATINA

Couples all looking and looking.
T.V. talking and listening.
Dusty antennas. Dirt may be copper.

Slowly they did not begin to hear. Some did not begin
to hear for a long time. Slowly some did not begin to
hear for a long time. Now now. Even now. Now and even
them. Older women went up and down in their disciplined
affairs with what the French call retinue doing as they
do. And do they do so? So they do.

We feel we feel. Feel so much. So much a feel. Feeling
for it, no oyster closer.

Why is there a dinner? Why is there a dimmer?
Why is there so much brilliant suffering? Why is there.
Shell me ouch. A hurt what is a hurt. A hurt is what
hides each one to seek. Beseech. Son of a bitch.
Steps up, many steps up, more and many many more.

Bunions are what hardening leaves behind what could be

soft if there were as many light steps in men as women. Insteps, stone steps, half steps, umbrella steps. Women and men.

For a very long time everybody shifts weight and then almost without a pause everybody steps. All steps are the same except composition which is balance going up or down all steps are different. Banister between the ears.

We step up as if to balance. Balance is not there. It is going to be there and we are here. This requires some step up for us naturally.

Escalate a little cheese. Tray brings irrigation. Everyone is taking returning. Hole in a mold. Moldy hole. Legs are all used. Armrests.

Once I was very full of convictions then that was over. Over stated. Underfed. Lost in talk, look, listen, love found I do tremendously. Dream trend us ly. Three men does free. Pardon me. What is the purpose of not keeping it in like it would never show? Hello is a necessary science. Take two.

Genesis

Adam's ridiculustrated apple turnover

puff adderevening delectable tartuffe.

You want it much as I do. Whose ear

but the wind and trees

       lying around doing nothing

Nothing doing.

       scaling the time when we were

and you caught my by the tail and me wiggling

before god and yesterday's hookuprooted

here through these bushmasters.

       A rose is a rose

don't give Adamn, talking about a coat

with beautiful colors like Joseph,

only a dreamer can understandard time: an hour

throws you offshooting the market to market

to buy a fat pigmentality.

      Tick- the salt's in

my earmark, an Oedipal footbridgehead

           inland of promise

me the moon I'll circle round the earthpea,

          nine days old-

not like they used to and us

moving like we're going somewherry up the Thames

into mercantilly-valley.

      Thy rod

it comforts me.

      Put 2 bucks in the field and sweet

David harping on Bathsheba,

sea opening up as many comeonsnakeyes

mountains underneath as there are C.I.A

to counter scale leaf's thin membrane dividing

to be or not answers.

Here comes a big one,

            look out sun!

Cheapcheaper by the dozen

birds piping stars flickering out every nightcap.

ONE DAY IT'S THE WIND

One day it's the wind tacking between cypresses
and hills heeling on sky til you're almost yanked
down alleys of cobblestones shoulder to shoulder
houses straddle the hills joy of hiking the bitte
schön herr doktor danke schön doktor roads
Miriam and Fruma scooped out of yesterday
out of dreams of life perpetuated in many different
languages and conjugated into the desert of chance
in a century of too much looking away now back
unafraid amid a bacchanal of cats high on air
on Jerusalem. From the balcony the old city winks
through the fat eyelid of the centuries and we
smile back at David and Solomon and laugh and
laughter fills the star soaked air

Now ramiis forth the joy of drilling
which is hammering on the sky. Aspirin!
it cries. Roof ! Roof ! barks the street
at a house from the anglo saxon hus
from hydan to hide and from growing linkage

our hide but where is that roof where

all aims are clear? Hinging a stone's

throw keeping the open door open and

see out of Erol's thin line of light

a window open and shalom come in

the washer dryer upstairs near the tiny

bedrooms. The rapid delicate cycle

reminds me of life and to breathe

the desert from here to Moab you gulp

L'chaim Henry Alicia Victor and Samara!

ANTARCTICA

One can not stray too far in the triangle
of the cold on the continent of an edge
and the nearest oceanic approach to God
600 miles across Drake Straits from Tierre del
Fuego to the tip of (English) Graham (American) Palmer
Peninsula–already the flags hang out
hyphenated only by the sea for there is no current
to break what it was they were searching. West winds'
tug? Come in qua qua of pelagic sea birds

It seemed the moon
blizzard into which he crawled
half key long the mile thick ice shelf
thins toward the coasts discharges
into the surrounding seas flat topped
ice bergs 10,000 would never sum up
how many dog sleds, sno-cat tractors,
arthropods and whales made the ice echo above
the volcanos resonating deep beneath it

For just as cyclones on the polar front loom

suddenly optimism stands out

Shackelton would go! That ridge of bedrock

was his spine. Southward, Endurance, from

Liutpold Coast. Ship struck, crushed, abandoned

28 men on an ice floe drift 457 days

Wilkins. Byrd reverses his wings and goes

South. Maps glaciers and the escarpment to the east

of Queen Maud mountains seen for 100 to 200 miles

100 below and they came. Eyes on stakes

Resupply point for German raiders

in the South Pacific. Antarcticas

stamped by seals, Falklands, came

like ice-breaking ships shepherding

cargo through the pack ice, go!

The new, ascent and the sun glisten

on plankton chowder and on few inch thick seams

coal ranges from lignite to anthracite

THE NOVEL OF DURING

But what of ?

Of what ?

From where you at.

Across the by.

Off it !

Except why ?

Because out.

In spite of between beneath ?

Because of between during !

But between during past ! And from since until beyond, and except for among during our into, throughout our entire within, without !

Without until among ? Until across or according to off on an out ?

Down and out ! Down past throughout.

Out and out down throughout ?

Over with. Out! Out with after ! Out despite against ! Over because from underneath in spite of against towards before, from underneath, across my beyond out. Out ! Out ! Out! Inside out !

TEETH, TENTACLES, AND SOME BLUE ENAMELED SCALES

To all you anglers of the world, thanks

a lot. After such a thunderous chain

of intro kudos, I can hardly wait to hear

what I've got to say myself. Although a surface

scratch–lights, please–I have wriggling on the line

if I can find this millions-of-years-old African fish

slide, Ah! See with only one lung, this lung fish

breathes air, paddles mud puddles, thanks

to its leggy fins tempting us to line

them up with the amphibians and the Radio City chain.

Rockettes, they're not. Although it can surface

to breathe, at best, a lung fish is the hard of hearing

cousin of the rhipidistians, those victims, last heard

of by the amphibians to which they had given rise. Fish,

please. Note here the gentle art of disappearing into the surface

by the pint-sized French Grunt: grey at night, its stripes thank

sunny day for small prey and crustaceans in the West Indian
  chain

of waters.Let puffers bluff it, these skinny pearls snake the line

 of greedier resistance by trading on the inhouse line

of the sea cucumber's intestines. So it isn't Boesky they hear

as much as the incessant flushing of the chain

of Canaries whose ubiquitous seas fork up daily specials for
  even gold fish.

Now catch this hammerhead. See how he smacks mollusks and
  thanks

his bloody nose for bass tossed between reefs and turquoise
  surface

And not a bone in his body! But eye his knife-life surface,

his cut and dry smile as if he were being picked out in a line

up. Like to frisk him? Next, please. No thanks.

Hey, catch this grouper grooving to the encrusted tuba on the
  starfish. Hear

today? Wan tomorrow. And tomorrow as if spat out by that
    Willy boy fish

and here still hatching is this 6-8 day embryonic chain

straight out of their father's mouth, a helter skelter chain

of bubbling tilapia. Startled. Their pinkish silver almost
    transparent as the surface

of these jellied eggs guarded by the Brazilian discus fish.

En guarde h'or deuvres! Lunging into a 40 yard line

dash, the small fry are gone! Chewed up in the Machiavellian
    ear

of this Moray eel. See how his camouflaged coils thank

the corals. Thankfully, a wind clears the surface.

Folks, you who are chained to the line

and hear the waves, put a fly on your rod. Now go fish!

PLEASE

did
you
see
a
little
about
so
high
an
adorable
a
on
his
just
opened
the
we're
new
to
where
were
you
sit!

HARK THE CLARK

for CLARK COOLIDGE

Hiccupping bees in the gosh flowers

and a trowel by Claus baileys a wick

in the Pepsi barnum. Shit up gravel

Have you no spokes? Imperial fart

of the dragon's snap—excuse

me! I've got loadenjitus

Feeling like you're on not in

Another difference between

the grande hotel o le petit

is simultaneous translation

into foreign currency hand out

Seine, thank you and you, Triomphe

scaffolding wrapped up like a Christo

And you crystal fountains spouting

Rond De Pointe pines sideswiped

by lights, snow and gold balls

bouncing as if out of happiness

in the human face

A plan

wholly mothered takes your arms

along gangplanks of ache and

shifts to his sewing on the button if

but the letter and I wedge between the

mountains, see batteries, botchless pen

and the cold drop cherry spies on

      Uncompassed. And intermittently swayed

      the shrubs and trees. More sky than earth.

      A white rain stitches the grey air and

      the heater hums

How

I can remember mighty well hearing about some kicked

out because they had gone and try hard as they could to

find work couldn't. Just because they had gone. But to

investigate, what's wrong with that? To ask what you

want and try to find out how you want to live. Some

went. Shall we subtract from them who didn't have any

what might be added all around? Now to the extend you

ask me where I was on such and such I'm supposed to

remember when I can hardly remember what all this has

to do with where I was when I was. Lots were. You have

to remember that thinking was different. About how

you saw what you thought was different. Right now

around us can you see what's happening? Can you see

over there some are shooting and some are hiding and

some are burning and some hit who aren't even in it

and here we are right on top of it and who agrees about

what it means? Some say it is because some itch to burn

to fuel without which what we have can't continue

while others say continue what? That we cannot

continue in this because we will always itch always burn. No

others say you cannot let such and such go on to grab

all he can, threaten to grab more, rape as he goes while

others say how come no one noticed that by building up

what he needed to rape and grab was the go ahead to

do the very what we are fighting now. True someone

says we have reached this and now we have to ask our

selves where do we go from here. But because we were

walking backwards shall we continue backwards all

depends on where you want to go and of course how

you get there is where you'll arrive.

VENUE

Yes out there you looking for the key

minimal wonderful foreign exchange

of character complex axiomatic faculties

withdraw like a rake in the rockery

intimacy accentuated by the inevitable

fissures of the sky and fuchsias cascading

from urns at a tilt as if distorted

by the pressures of intense seeing

fire us into being like a cast

iron skillet to shoot the rapids

of a two seater feeling pour quaff

Monsieur and the coming of the multiples

with peace to the top in the given up dark

WAVES

Beep beep beep honks

the kid at the no snow

squeaking towel basket

lady all the preterit

that's left on the beach

of a five year old birthday

balloons into the sky fishnet

come-on of squid, quiddities

and the thock and thock and

thock like an axe on wood

a cappella of scavengers

as if crests all queued

in only one direction crabs

pelicans and now a seagull

wipes its feet on the moon Shit!

Hahaha's the crow top of the

tropical pine threading the sea

through its needles knot among

of greens the aqua colada shuttles

into the bougainvillea grooved noon

NEW CITY

Sometimes its quiet comes on the eye sets off the door

chameleon also a big bee in the bedroom later when he's

fighting to get out all on the same principle so you've

been called many times so what do you do I'm coming

into the house see which eye gave me the signal are there

breakins a lot puts iron between the wall and comes out

against professional burglars you can't do this in 10

minutes he can deterrent is either coming in one door

downstairs with another person too complicated front

vestibule leave open til the end of this year better to

chip in for a guard

COLLAPSAR, ACHERNAR, PARASHAH

If when two motion away from each

light emitted by one will the other

shifted end hubble the stars

and from earth exhibit the shifting

recessional crease increasing idly

light spectrum earth receives no

longer duce human eye in the blue

grass night agree that this red

in the dark accepted the speed of

and not galaxy live for consequence

of the fixed light any object farther

15 billion light years even if

galaxies light from had time to are

aging and their finite lives of

light pump into verse the bright

points of distant Edgar Allan a

radiation field static nonexpanding

ferret the far too sky prods

11^{1/2}

What was the long looked forward coming to
rain on the bleachers the termites carried off
in the hide of the teachers' strike
you oddly that summer
caught a highfly, no balls.

Splinters still being tweezed
as possibilities of the big board rub against the grain.
What plank to assume and supphose
that necessary mesh to fill in,
your legs never felt more comfy.

Moon and sun go down between the leaves
you in this humid atmosphere
giving yourself to someone.
This is a trust. But are you equal to it?
Credit my account with that smile
was very warm. Now that too is gone.

All that remains is a low sky, the rain
is changing to snow.

WAR AND PEACE

Well perhaps you were being sandbagged

at Anna Pavlovna's soiree ten feet deep

as some March night when winter resumes its sway

of a controlled press and what has been approved

scatters its last snows and storms its desperate fury

with a serene expression on military commands hardened

to protect itself against suffering concessions

that are a propaganda victory to high density

smiles and this occurred every time she mentioned her
  illustrious

bottom floor or down under it and why we were going

topics ended and time had come for intimate conversation

to ensure detonation fused only in the tail because no fuse

greeted him with the nod accorded to the roving bands

of execution squads to search out deserters and notices

here a spindle that has stopped or there one that

captured them the most headlines were what turned out

shoulders and popped his buttons to batter morale even the
    sinewy

expressed forgiveness of his indiscretion nodded and said

as procurement accelerated again in the late

revenge before the television cameras could not conceal

the dug in positions that a footman was helping into

the carriage of the future on an empty stomach always

conscious in that desert of increasing high and middle clouds

to keep the enemy in doubt about exact allied dispositions

head off some chemical attacks by moving quickly forward so

much exasperated with one another and long after the action
    had

begun drinks he offered they ferment while we drive

SALOOP

Iambic plenary allegretto to the fragrant

of the univalent static of amiable

and to the repugnant for which it stank

one natty underdeveloped go-go

with libidinous and justifiable for all

BY THE BEAUTIFUL C

What need have we
of needles because
we all make our own

sandwiches and there
are no thimbles
and how we arrive

comes to us. No
know thimbles and
how we arrive comes

to us. Case this.
A very course. A
very course cases

the arriving
that sandwiches
turning around

something sweet
and hold the
consequences.

PINES

And you blue why chirp yesterday when

the sun hollers like a man was deaf

eats with its pumpkin open! bursts

like the coach for want of a fuse on the

junior high field at the girl's team Ready

for the pitch? Thunk. Out. Paradise

may not be perfect. Out of the fly

raking attendance: Cut Japanese maples?

Present. White nose crow? Caha. Gabriella

Johanna windmilling her two tooth present

at the window makes me dissolve and for what

On rotten apples in the yellow grass ants

are marching with their doglike insouciance

 And suckled of its pink delight why

 freak any leaf that is not for flight?

COMBINATIONS

Another round, ladies and gentlemen.

Cast your bets. As dice are to the poet,

so to the paper, that calculated line in

which getting lost, find yourself

a distant clam to pry it open. Ladyfingers!

Why play? Why not lounge around in palazzo

pajamas sheer violet to the afternoon and eat

kumquats? Bowing, bending like some eunuch

in a harem. It's the old story- in a few

hours, you get hungry.

Is Madame shooting? Of course it's a matter

of choice. Your talent lies in your selection.

There is no abstract art. You must always

start with something. Afterward you can

remove all traces of reality. There's no

danger then because the idea of the

object will have left an indelible mark.

This morning's yellow light, for example,

sticks as so much tartar between the teeth

scraping the edges of the carpet where the

smallest flowers claw at the border like

red leopard paws. It took a family seven

years to weave this Kerman. Children have

gone blind knotting 250 threads to a

square inch. What's the point?

In all games played with dice, rolled in

such a way that they will turn at random

in the air. Then come to rest on some

flat surface. The combination of the topmost

surfaces of the dice decides according to

some predetermined pattern, whether the

player wins, or having lost, to reconsider

the odds.

6 combinations will produce a 7. There are

30 others that will not. So the odds of

your casting a 7, are 5 to 1 against you.

Yet the week winds you up in a toboggan

on Grenoble banking on seconds. And all

the skiers faster than I can record them.

Is it that you doubt the snow? What with

all the distant peaks thumbs up sucking

the wind. What a bite! But beginning to

warm up on this deck, the sun like an orange

dripping in my mouth. Here, take this section.

Perhaps the earliest gaming implements

equivalent to dice were knucklebones.

A juicy consideration, your hands digging up

in Chinese excavations early as 600 B.C. dice

used for forecasting tomorrow. And what kind of

a day has it been?

A line along which warm air has been lifted

by the actions of opposing edges of cold air.

Precipitation requiring two umbrella steps.

But come in, you'll catch pneumonia!

Your dress soaked to the skin with all

the transparent inconsistencies that are

meaning to show up breasts but coming out

snake eyes. Pot luck to have rooted behind

the window, that coleus just stretched and grew.

As for yoga. Getting in touch with your toes

or how your back could feel cramped from

this position so long like the life of

each word depended upon it. Relax. Take a

bath.

Actually, I've never does this before.

Although I'm not going to fracture my

head like Glenn did. Pass the soap.

Would you mind scrubbing my back? Ah

I feel like a new woman in a poem that

just changed my life. Hand me the towel.

I'll be dry in a second. But don't peek.

I'd much rather surprise you.

MIRIAM

a claustrophobic tri-syllabic countdown from the Hebrew

mir yam rebellion festering in a hum. But this mm, a

consonantal boomerang on the melancholy scale of a mur

mur that long O's Moses into orbit but has Miriam

coming and going inflames an ir/i/am aching to be free

into an ir/i/rush toward a magnetically sagging um. And

this so murkingly deflects off tooth pasted irium and

mir mir on the um as if am is never to be so as to make

a generative mockery of that prophecy timbrelled so long

ago singing and dancing at the Red Sea.

HOMAGE

The sky for and 20 blackbirds

The sky of mountainous atmosphere of mind at sea

The sky of bushy browed Beethoven

The sky under De Gaulle

The inconsistent sky

The infectious sky

The sky ringing long distance

The sky high on poppies

The sky sensibly priced

The sky bobsledding white water

The sky in the style of Louis XIV

The sky was bruised by Nijinsky

The sky the shadow knows

The shear fuzz sky

The sky pilling always

The sky poses for Coca-Cola

The sky strips for Magritte

The sky is riddled with holes

The sky branches out in ellipses

The vitamin C sky

The sky at eye level rather than high like a chandelier

The sky shaded by faces

The sky smokes Benson and hedges

The sky inspired drag

The Oscar Wilde sky

The sky drunk behind bars

The more to come sky

The sky idling spring

The sky wild about you

The sky curries the earth and stews in its juices

The sky eats with its mouth open

The sky careening with crotch and foxglove

The tanglewood sky

The sky is not the sky

The Jewish sky

The sky of the ghost of the messiah

The sky of Turner burning London's harbor

The sky lilacs impaled

The sky spiralling loosed leaf

The sky blind Ophelia

The sky rick rack of pines

The sky losing its hem

The kamikaze sky

The sky show on the road with no angels

The sky on the queues piano piano

The cyclops sky

The sky at ceiling zero

The windexed sky

The sky of a tin man sideways

The sky mothering pearl

The sky flies on one wing

The sky purls one and casts off

FROM 1000 FATHOMS

Athens driving rain. Atlantic

City treading 40 feet waves. Amsterdam

waves back. Through arctic wattle Bangkok

weaves. Beijing flakes. Bermuda save frigid

air during rainy patches, hail. Raw Brussels.

Cold snaps Budapest. Rain volleys the

Brahmaputra, a gargling scene Bonn. Roll

out the barrel Buffalo. For Cairo's a jolly

good fellow. It rain and snow Caracas.

Casablanca wrap-around snow. Deck the halls

Chicago. Columbus bitter. Cincinnati knocked

cold and Colorado Springs! Because record low

blows Dublin like De Moines squalls Fargo? A

below freezing Helsinki snows Johannesburg

under. London hobbled. Small craft bash Manilla.

No shortage cloud covers Moscow. New Delhi digging

out. Oklahoma stranded. Stand by Orlando as Paris

trough packs Providence powder. Rome watch your

nose! Sydney throw another log on. Clouds

that shower Tokyo Venice here they come. Winnipeg

where are you! Zanzibar get out your blowers

and crank!

VIBRATING

for HENRY SOLAN

on one hand the mind the world on the other and her lips
which she fed him beneath a lemon tree in a ripe disquisition
that he enter again

If Morning Star was a whore Hidalgo had not yet won the
lottery which nibbled at him like a worm against the high-
way of the sky a little worn at the knuckles from rubbing
against uncultivated fields wild anemones and on the knees
of his memories celibating himself like a tenor in longing but
also of some bliss as if the margins of could were also being
realized

You're not going to jump he said out the window she
could not see so shy he asked for her noun and address just
broken up and would she like to Daiquiri loved to around
the floor of pink candlelit tables closer to the band in her off
the shoulder feeling he could hang on her lower lip for an
evening buoyant with words and only hands and thighs to
disperse them and a hunch of tulips like life was a riddle of
crevices and voluptuous uncertainty bellying the interstices of
whether

TROISGROS

for SUSAN KOMAROW

What an island
of a salad!
leafy as a trade wind
just the waves to wake
raddichio up hopping
with lobster garlic
coconut knocked off
the French chef's
twelve year stint
in Brazil and extradited
by the light
raspberry vinaigrette
delicate yet nutty
as a hunch, Houdini, sun
flower seed, Red
Grooms' New York's
subway's rush
into morning. Svelte
mango juicy as a tango
by Susan Rinaldi

slicing into it

the hip twist

of quince and black

mustard seed. The

rough and the smooth

–without film noir–a

compass of unstrung

possibility: from the east

a gingery snip

to the nussli where

Switzerland is

Crisp as the snow

tangy and mellow

as cilantro

birthday weather

personified isn't it

just the present to

toast the present of

providence with? Echo the

years and eat them? Clawed

drizzled long shot candle

lit returns heaped high wind

tossed green

AND ALL ITS INCARNATIONS

Why I do it if it's I who do it maybe I

is only a yawn between penned up thighs to

slip prolific into the instant

swamp of photo opportunities and sound

bites onto the higher ground against

great gulps of habit. Death is watching.

Fortunately the opening passed my flaps

is not superficial on my tiniest tongue.

Shall I post notice? Key the animal?

Perhaps it's paradise with nine minutes

left to play. In the basket shots come

and go. Darling you're like shooting

fish in a barrel. Delicious obscurity

of a hard cup, shall I allay from the rear?

Tear the sky from its unicorn I am only

riding a cloud.

SPACETIMEMATTER

Which causative which reflexive

bunches and lets again upside down

and pouring doesn't suffer magnitude

in translation but riddles around

the night stem silence dark vast

pit instant swept away

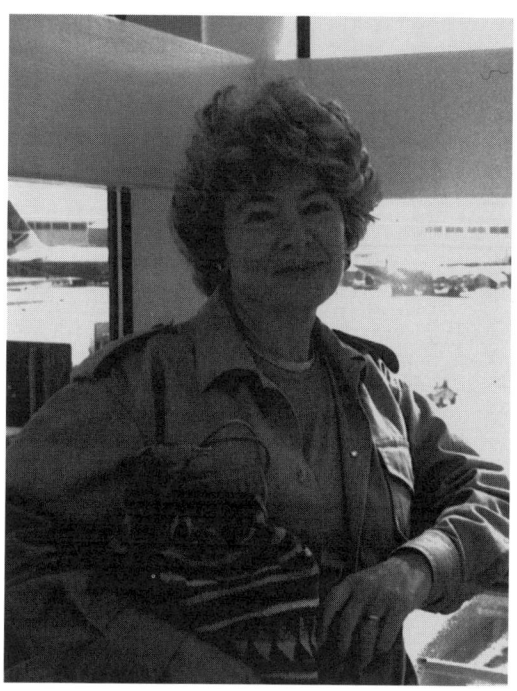

Miriam Solan

A native New Yorker, Solan completed her B.A. and M.F.A. (1981) at Sarah Lawrence College where she studied with Grace Paley.

She has taught poetry workshops at the New Lincoln and Bentley schools in Manhattan. Her poems have been choreographed and performed at The Cubiclo, La Mama, and Theater of the Open Eye, in New York City, as well as in college venues.

She has read her poems widely and they have been published in many literary journals including *Poetry New York*, *The World*, *East Coast Anthology*, *lingo*, *Torque*, as well as in the anthology *For A Living* published by the University of Illinois Press.

Married and mother of two daughters, Miriam Solan lives in suburban New York.

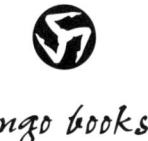

lingo books

Home In Three Days. Don't Wash.
Linda Smukler

Little Men
Kevin Killian

Tilt
Gillian McCain

A Woman Combing
Miriam Solan

Series Editor: Jonathan Gams